GREA_
RACEHORSES

TRIPLE CROWN WINNERS AND OTHER CHAMPIONS

JOHN GREEN

DOVER PUBLICATIONS
GARDEN CITY, NEW YORK

For thousands of years, human beings have staged and watched horse races, often betting on the outcome. The sport is thought to have originated among nomadic tribesmen of Central Asia, where the horse was domesticated around 4500 B.C.E. Horse racing was highly popular among the ancient Greeks and Romans; they also enjoyed horse-and-chariot races. Today, horse racing involves competitions between thoroughbred horses over tracks ranging from three-quarters of a mile to two miles. In America, it is one of the most popular spectator sports, along with football, baseball, basketball, and NASCAR racing. This book features 30 detailed line drawings of some of the greatest racehorses of all time, presented in chronological order—including all thirteen winners of the Triple Crown, listed below in bold. And each realistic, ready-to-color illustration is accompanied by a brief summary of the horse's life and accomplishments on the racetrack.

List of Illustrations

Bibliographical Note
Great Racehorses: Triple Crown Winners and Other Champions, first published by Dover Publications in 2016, is a revised and updated version of *Great Racehorses,* originally published by Dover in 2007. The book has been updated to include Justify.

International Standard Book Number
ISBN-13: 978-0-486-80716-4
ISBN-10: 0-486-80716-9

Manufactured in the United States of America
80716907   2023
www.doverpublications.com

1. Sir Barton. The first horse to win what would become known as the Triple Crown of American horse racing, Sir Barton was born in 1916 in Kentucky. He was sold in 1918 to a Canadian businessman who entrusted his training to H. Guy Bedwell and jockey Johnny Loftus. They entered Sir Barton in the 1919 Kentucky Derby, expecting to use him as a pacemaker for another horse—the highly regarded Billy Kelly. To their surprise, however, the chestnut colt led the entire race and won by five lengths. Just four days later, Sir Barton was in Baltimore where he won the Preakness. The following month he won the Belmont Stakes easily, becoming the first winner of the Triple Crown.

2. Man O' War. Known as "Big Red," this legendary chestnut stallion is considered by many the greatest racehorse in history. Born in 1917 he won 20 of his 21 races, shattering course records and coming in second just once, to a horse named Upset. Man O' War retired to a successful 27-year stud career, siring 64 stakes winners and the Triple Crown winner, War Admiral.

3. Gallant Fox. Winner of the Triple Crown in 1930, the bay colt Gallant Fox raced for only two seasons (1929–30), winning 11 of 17 starts. His winnings of $308,275 as a three-year-old stood as a single season record for 17 years. Born in 1927, Gallant Fox lived to be twenty-seven years old. The horse is buried at Claiborne Farm, Kentucky, where he was born.

4. Omaha. The son of 1930 Triple Crown winner Gallant Fox, Omaha was foaled at the famous Claiborne Farm in Paris, Kentucky. He was a big colt, with a white blaze on his forehead. Omaha was the second favorite in the 1935 Kentucky Derby and despite cold weather and heavy rain, he won by a length and a half with his jockey not having to use the whip. A week later he was the favorite at the Preakness and he won that easily—by six lengths. Finally, on June 8th, 1935, on a sloppy track on Long Island, Omaha edged out Firethorn to win the third leg of the Triple Crown.

5. Seabiscuit. The subject of a bestselling book and an acclaimed motion picture, Seabiscuit was a grandson of the great Man O' War. Born in 1933, he displayed his heritage of speed and toughness by becoming the first horse to top $400,000 in winnings. Of the 89 races he entered, the horse earned 33 wins, 15 second places, and 13 thirds. His defeat of War Admiral in a 1938 match race ranks as one of the greatest victories in American racing history.

6. War Admiral. A son of the legendary Man O' War, War Admiral was born at Faraway Farm in Lexington, Kentucky, in 1934. Although not as big as his famous sire, he did inherit his father's fiery temperament and racing ability. War Admiral won twenty-one of his twenty-six starts, including all three Triple Crown races in 1937. He was voted the 1937 Horse of the Year, narrowly beating out his nephew, the celebrated Seabiscuit.

7. Whirlaway. Born in 1938 at Calumet farm in Kentucky, Whirlaway was a chestnut colt trained by Ben A. Jones and ridden by the legendary Eddie Arcaro, the only jockey to win two Triple Crowns. He won the 1941 Kentucky Derby by a record-tying eight lengths, and then proceeded to win both the Preakness and the Belmont Stakes, earning himself a place in the pantheon of Triple Crown winners.

8. Count Fleet. Sired by 1928 Kentucky Derby winner Reigh Count, Count Fleet was a slow starter as a two-year-old, losing several times before finally winning a race. As a three-year-old, however, he dominated the racing world, never losing a race. Count Fleet won the 1943 Kentucky Derby by three lengths, the Preakness by eight lengths, and the Belmont Stakes by an unheard of twenty-five lengths! He is today regarded as one of the all-time great thoroughbred horses. Count Fleet was retired because of injury and did not race as a four-year-old. He enjoyed great success as a sire and lived to the ripe old age of thirty-three.

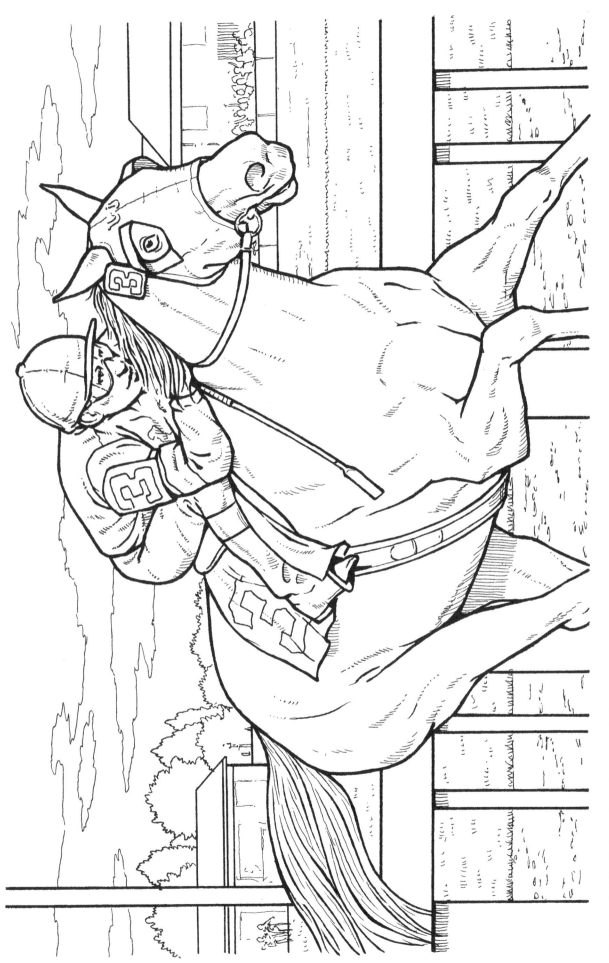

9. Assault. Foaled at the King Ranch in Texas in 1943, Assault remains the only Texas-bred Triple Crown winner. He was trained by the legendary Hall-of-Famer Max Hirsch, who soon sensed something special in the colt. Unfortunately, Assault was plagued by illness and injury; as a youngster he stepped on a stake that penetrated his right hoof. The hoof was permanently deformed and Assault developed a slight limp. However, the "Club-footed Comet," as he came to be called, showed no signs of a disability while at full gallop and he would decisively win all three of the 1946 Triple Crown races, becoming just the seventh horse to achieve that feat.

10. Citation. Winner of 19 of 20 races in his first two seasons, this speedy bay colt, born in 1945, won the Triple Crown in 1948. Not only did he win all three races, he won them easily by comfortable margins. It was not until Secretariat in 1973 that another horse would win the elusive Triple Crown. Citation eventually passed the one million dollar mark in winnings at the advanced (for a racehorse) age of six.

11. Neji. Named for a Rudyard Kipling character, Neji was a chestnut gelding, born in 1950. Trained as a jumper, Neji became one of the greatest American steeplechasers of the twentieth century—a three-time national steeplechase champion. At 4, Neji won the Brook Steeplechase Handicap and earned a second place finish in the Grand National. He was also named Steeplechase Horse of the Year for 1955. At 7 Neji was named Steeplechase Champion after winning the Grand National.

12. Nashua. Foaled in 1952, this bay colt grew into a large, imposing stallion. His charisma and the fact that he was a bit of a ham endeared him to racing fans. As a two-year-old in 1954, Nashua entered eight races, winning six and finishing second twice, a performance that earned him champion two-year-old honors. In 1956 Nashua won his famous match race with the great thoroughbred Swaps, who had defeated him in the 1955 Kentucky Derby. Upon the death of his owner, William Woodward Jr., Nashua was sold and bought for a record price of over $1,250,000.

13. Kelso. One of the finest and fastest geldings in American racing history, Kelso, born in 1957, was Horse of the Year for five years running, from 1960 to 1964. The only horse to claim that distinction, he was also the leading all-time money winner of his day, having come close to the two million dollar level. As he traveled around the country from race to race, he always had a dog for a companion, and was supplied with specially bottled Arkansas spring water.

14. Buckpasser. Born in 1963, this bay colt was not only a classically beautiful thoroughbred with no physical flaws, he was friendly, gentle, and easy to handle. His grandfather on his mother's side was the great War Admiral. After winning the Arlington Classic in 1966, Buckpasser went on a fifteen-race winning streak, including the American Derby (he broke the track record), the Chicago Stakes, and the grueling two-mile-long Jockey Club Gold Cup.

15. Red Rum. A bay gelding, this beloved British racehorse was born in 1965. He achieved an unmatched historic first when he won the Grand National in 1973, 1974 and 1977 while coming in second in 1975 and 1976. A favorite of the people, "Rummy" became a national celebrity, appearing at supermarket openings and annually leading the Grand National parade. His likeness graced playing cards, mugs, posters, models, paintings, plates, and jigsaw puzzles.

16. Nijinsky II. Foaled in Canada in 1967, Nijinsky II was named after the famous Russian dancer, Vaslav Nijinsky. The horse's sire was Northern Dancer, one of the greatest of all Canadian thoroughbred racehorses. In 1970, Nijinsky II won five major races, including the Epsom Derby and the Irish Sweeps Derby. In fact, over the course of his brilliant racing career, the bay colt smashed the European earnings record. He was subsequently syndicated for a world record sum.

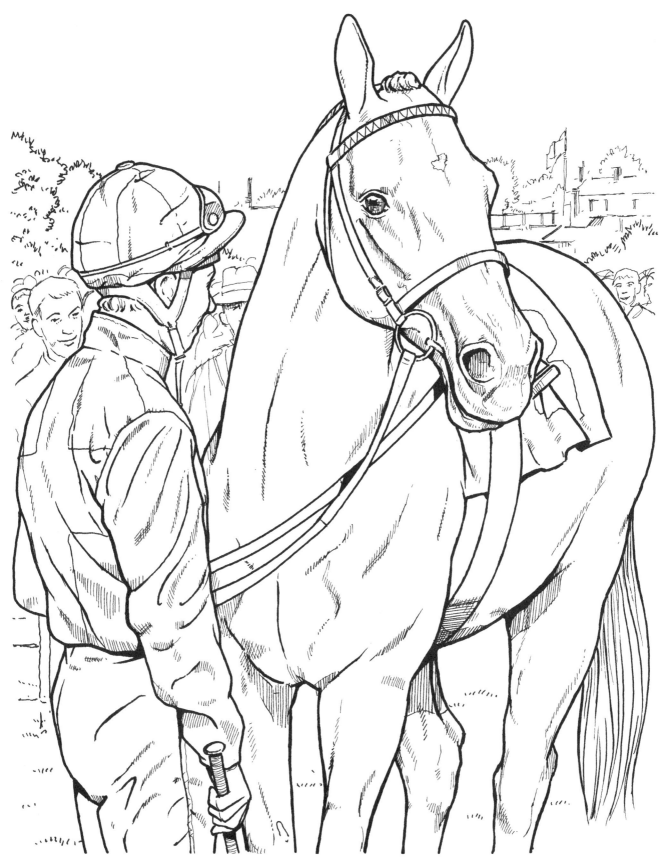

17. Mill Reef. Born in 1968, Mill Reef was owned and bred by the American financier Paul Mellon. Early on it was thought that the horse would do better on turf courses in Europe rather than American dirt tracks, so Mill Reef was sent to England. There he developed into an outstanding middle distance thoroughbred. In one year alone (1971) he won the Epsom Derby, the Eclipse Stakes, the King George VI & Queen Elizabeth Diamond Stakes at Ascot, and the Prix de l'Arc de Triomphe.

18. Brigadier Gerard. One of the greatest milers in British racing history, the bay colt Brigadier Gerard, foaled in 1968, won seventeen out of his eighteen races. He was voted Champion Miler for 1971 and named Horse-Of-The-Year for 1971 and 1972. At four, Brigadier Gerard ran his unbeaten streak to 15 with wins in the Lockinge Stakes, Westbury Stakes, Prince of Wales's Stakes, Eclipse Stakes, and King George VI & Queen Elizabeth Diamond Stakes.

19. Secretariat. Sired by the American champion Bold Ruler, Secretariat was born in 1970. He grew into a huge chestnut colt with blazing speed. In 1973, after winning the Kentucky Derby and the Preakness, the stage was set for Secretariat to win the Belmont Stakes, and with it, the Triple Crown. In one of the most spectacular races ever, Secretariat completely outclassed the field, winning the Belmont by an unheard-of 31 lengths. His time of 2 minutes, 24 seconds slashed 2.6 seconds off the old record. By the time he retired, the champion thoroughbred had compiled a record of 16 wins in 21 starts.

20. Seattle Slew. A husky, powerful dark brown colt, nearly black in color, Seattle Slew was born in 1974. In 1977, after an unbroken string of victories, he became the tenth winner of the American Triple Crown. Moreover, he was the only horse to win the series while still undefeated. In the course of his career, Seattle Slew won 14 of 17 races, and earned $1,208,726. In 1981, this great champion was elected to the National Museum and Racing Hall of Fame.

21. Affirmed. Winner of the Triple Crown in 1978, and the first horse to register two million dollars in earnings, the chestnut colt Affirmed, born in 1975, is remembered for his neck-and-neck battles with his great rival, Alydar. Although Affirmed usually won, Alydar was always a close second. Their classic duel in the 1978 Belmont Stakes (won by Affirmed by a nose) is considered one of the greatest horse races in American history.

22. John Henry. This dark bay gelding, foaled in 1975, was named after the American folk hero. The horse was ornery and prone to bite, but a very successful racehorse. Of the 89 races he started, he won 39. By comparison, Seabiscuit started the same number of races, but won only 33. John Henry twice won the Eclipse Award as Horse of the Year, and was inducted into racing's Hall of Fame in 1990. Over a long career, he earned $6,497, 947, retiring in 1985 as the world's richest thoroughbred.

23. Spectacular Bid. Tom Meyerhoff, a wealthy Baltimore construction executive, bought the gray yearling colt, born in 1976, for a modest $37,000 because the horse had a slightly turned leg. It was a wise investment. Spectacular Bid went on to win twenty-six of his thirty races, including the first two legs of the American Triple Crown in 1979. Over the course of his career, he earned more than two million dollars.

24. Bold 'n Determined. This bay filly, foaled in 1977, had a persona that perfectly matched her name. Small, robust and strong, she was all business and required a great deal of attention. As a two-year-old, she was unbeaten in 4 starts. At three, she won 9 of her 12 races. Overall, out of 20 starts, she won 16, and earned over $900,000.

25. Shergar. Born in 1978, this bay colt proved to be one of the greatest middle-distance horses ever to race in England. Between 1981 and 1982 he won the Epsom Derby by a record ten lengths, notched another ten-length win in the Guardian Classic Trial at Sandown, and a twelve-length victory in the Chester Vase. He also won the Irish Derby and the "King George." Unfortunately, Shergar was kidnapped from his owner's stud farm in 1983, and never seen again.

26. Desert Orchid. Foaled in 1979, this gray steeplechaser affectionately known as *Dessie* was one of the United Kingdom's most famous racehorses over jumps. Indeed, his breathtaking leaps were one of the most compelling sights in racing. By the time he retired in December 1991, he had won 34 of his 70 starts, including Ascot, the Whitbread Gold Cup, the Cheltenham Gold Cup, and many more. Over the course of his career, he amassed £654,066 in prize money. Desert Orchid is still fondly remembered by British racing fans.

27. Cigar. This bay colt was born in 1990 and became one of the finest racehorses in American track history. In 1995, he won all ten races he entered, including the Pimlico Special and the U.S. Breeders Cup Classic. This achievement won him the Eclipse Award as Horse of the Year. In 1996 he continued his winning ways, extending his winning streak to sixteen consecutive races, matching Citation's record. When he retired at the end of the 1996 season, Cigar was the richest racehorse in history, with earnings of $9,999,815.

28. Point Given. Nicknamed "The Big Red Train," this large, elegant chestnut colt was born in 1998. As a three-year-old, he won the Preakness Stakes and the Belmont Stakes, along with the Eclipse Award for Horse of the Year. He remains the only horse in his- tory to win four $1,000,000 races in a row. In one of them, the Belmont Stakes, he beat the times of both Affirmed and Seattle Slew. Out of 13 starts, he won 9 and came in second three times.

29. American Pharoah. A bay colt with a faint star on his forehead, American Pharoah won the Triple Crown in 2015. He became the first horse to achieve this since Affirmed in 1978—a thirty-eight year gap! American Pharoah's sire was Pioneerof the Nile, who came in second in the 2009 Kentucky Derby. He was trained by Bob Baffert and usually ridden by Victor Espinoza. He was owned during his racing career by Ahmed Zayat. American Pharoah came into his three-year-old racing season highly touted, and he did not disappoint. He won the Kentucky Derby by a length, the Preakness by seven lengths, and the Belmont by five and a half lengths, earning himself horse racing immortality in the process.

30. Justify. Defying two different precedents, the latest Triple Crown winner, Justify, accomplished the feat in 2018. First, a horse that hadn't raced prior to age two had never won the Triple Crown—and hadn't won the Kentucky Derby since 1882! Second, Justify retired without having lost a single race, prompted by an ankle injury. Justify was trained by Bob Baffert, as was his Triple Crown predecessor, American Pharoah. Justify followed in American Pharoah's hoofsteps and retired to Coolmore's Ashford Stud farm.